Greater Than a Tourist Book Series
Reviews from Readers

I think the series is wonderful and beneficial for tourists to get information before visiting the city.

-Seckin Zumbul, Izmir Turkey

I am a world traveler who has read many trip guides but this one really made a difference for me. I would call it a heartfelt creation of a local guide expert instead of just a guide.

-Susy, Isla Holbox, Mexico

New to the area like me, this is a must have!

-Joe, Bloomington, USA

This is a good series that gets down to it when looking for things to do at your destination without having to read a novel for just a few ideas.

-Rachel, Monterey, USA

Good information to have to plan my trip to this destination.

-Pennie Farrell, Mexico

Great ideas for a port day.

-Mary Martin USA

Aptly titled, you won't just be a tourist after reading this book. You'll be greater than a tourist!

-Alan Warner, Grand Rapids, USA

Even though I only have three days to spend in San Miguel in an upcoming visit, I will use the author's suggestions to guide some of my time there. An easy read - with chapters named to guide me in directions I want to go.

-Robert Catapano, USA

Great insights from a local perspective! Useful information and a very good value!

-Sarah, USA

This series provides an in-depth experience through the eyes of a local. Reading these series will help you to travel the city in with confidence and it'll make your journey a unique one.

-Andrew Teoh, Ipoh, Malaysia

GREATER THAN A TOURIST-ISTANBUL TURKEY

50 Travel Tips from a Local

Daiana M. Altinay

CZYK Publishing Since 2011.

Greater Than a Tourist
Visit our website at www.GreaterThanaTourist.com

Lock Haven, PA
All rights reserved.
ISBN: 9781793123664

>TOURIST

50 TRAVEL TIPS FROM A LOCAL

BOOK DESCRIPTION

Are you excited about planning your next trip?

Do you want to try something new?

Would you like some guidance from a local?

If you answered yes to any of these questions, then this Greater Than a Tourist book is for you.

Greater Than a Tourist- Istanbul, Turkey by Daiana M. Altinay offers the inside scoop on Istanbul. Most travel books tell you how to travel like a tourist. Although there is nothing wrong with that, as part of the Greater Than a Tourist series, this book will give you travel tips from someone who has lived at your next travel destination.

In these pages, you will discover advice that will help you throughout your stay. This book will not tell you exact addresses or store hours but instead will give you excitement and knowledge from a local that you may not find in other smaller print travel books.

Travel like a local. Slow down, stay in one place, and get to know the people and the culture. By the time you finish this book, you will be eager and prepared to travel to your next destination.

TABLE OF CONTENTS

DEDICATION

This book is dedicated to my husband Tunacan, who guided my journey to the inner soul of a city that had hooked me from the first encounter. Thanks to him and his wonderful family I feel that I can call now Istanbul my home.

ABOUT THE AUTHOR

Daiana is a Romanian girl, coming from the famous Transylvanian realms of Dracula, who realized at a tender age that the narrow little medieval passages of Bistrița, her hometown, were suffocating her, so she decided to leave home and find herself a big city. And she found two. After spending more than 15 years in Bucharest, capital of Romania, Daiana met Tunacan her husband, who is originally from Istanbul, Turkey. This encounter between the two of them came as no surprise for the people close to her, as she had always been mysteriously connected with Turkey and especially Istanbul. At the moment, the two of them are dividing their time between Bucharest and Istanbul, together with their two cats, Alfie and Pisica, and Pufi, the Samoyed dog.

A passionate writer, avid reader and dreamer about faraway places, Daiana loves to travel as often as possible, longing to discover exotic landscapes and interesting people.

HOW TO USE THIS BOOK

The Greater Than a Tourist book series was written by someone who has lived in an area for over three months. The goal of this book is to help travelers either dream or experience different locations by providing opinions from a local. The author has made suggestions based on their own experiences. Please do your own research before traveling to the area in case the suggested places are unavailable.

Travel Advisories: As a first step in planning any trip abroad, check the Travel Advisories for your intended destination.
https://travel.state.gov/content/travel/en/traveladvisories/traveladvisories.html

FROM THE PUBLISHER

Traveling can be one of the most important parts of a person's life. The anticipation and memories that you have are some of the best. As a publisher of the Greater Than a Tourist book series, as well as the popular 50 Things to Know book series, we strive to help you learn about new places, spark your imagination, and inspire you. Wherever you are and whatever you do I wish you safe, fun, and inspiring travel.

Lisa Rusczyk Ed. D.
CZYK Publishing

OUR STORY

Traveling is a passion of the "Greater than a Tourist" series creator. Lisa studied abroad in college, and for their honeymoon Lisa and her husband toured Europe. During her travels to Malta, an older man tried to give her some advice based on his own experience living on the island since he was a young boy. She was not sure if she should talk to the stranger but was interested in his advice. When traveling to some places she was wary to talk to locals because she was afraid that they weren't being genuine. Through her travels, Lisa learned how much locals had to share with tourists. Lisa created the "Greater Than a Tourist" book series to help connect people with locals. A topic that locals are very passionate about sharing.

WELCOME TO
> TOURIST

INTRODUCTION

"Istanbul…The constant beating
of the wave of the east against the
rock of the west…"

– Susan Moody

Why do certain places possess the power to wrap us in a multitude of invisible energetic cords and lure us towards them, nobody knows. I like to call these experiences soul connections or karmic callings or even better, a feeling of being home. Many of us have probably experienced at least once in life an inexplicable calling or longing for a place that we didn't know too much about or that we had just visited once. Although I tried to understand for long time my fascination with Istanbul, passing from past live experiences to déjà vu and soul searching, I could never quite completely gasp the mesmerizing fascination that this metropolis surrounds me with.

By writing this book I began an exploration of my inner self, a journey which I hope will guide you also in discovering, understanding and maybe even loving this city as much as I do.

1. UNITED NATIONS OF ISTANBUL

Istanbul is a city with a thousand and one faces, a fusion of cultures, ethnicities and beliefs. What has always fascinated me since living here is the opportunity of interacting with people from so many different cultural backgrounds and with such different perceptions about the day-to-day life, that you don't even need to travel anywhere else outside the city to feel that you're expanding your horizons. With a population of over 17 million residents it's quite difficult to bump into people that you know while you're walking around the streets, and this feeling is somehow liberating.

2. "THE CAT IN THE HAT " – DR. SEUSS

As a cat lover and proud owner of two of them, I was happy to discover the big affinity that people of Istanbul have towards their cats. Cats are not only in the hats, they are everywhere from streets and shops to hammams or restaurants. Cats are not considered animals, just Cats, a spoiled species with special rights of its own. You can even find here a famous female cat figure called Tombili, which was honored with a statue after her death. She became internationally known thanks to a photography of her while posing on the street in a very relaxed manner. If you are a cat lover and want to visit the statue you can find it at Zühtüpaşa Mahallesi, Güleç Çk No: 1, Kadikoy.

3. LITTLE LITTLE IN THE MIDDLE

When you visit Istanbul, you face a big risk of getting overfed. The locals find pleasure in tempting you with such a large choice of delicacies that it's almost impossible to resist. From vegetarians to carnivores and from food lovers to picky eaters, everybody will find its choice. When they go to a restaurant, locals like to order the entire menu in the middle of the table giving the opportunity for everybody to try a little from all the food choices. Faced with Kumpirs, Pides, Koftes, Kebabs, Mezes and Baklavas, little is the last thing you will be able to stick to.

Their gastronomy reaches superlative levels, no matter if you eat on the street or in a luxury restaurant. For an authentic ottoman experience I recommend you to try Pandele Restaurant inside the Spice Market, or Galata Evi a restaurant built inside a former British prison. The menu here is diverse serving a mixture of Turkish, Georgian and Russian dishes.

4. LOOK BEFORE YOU LEAP

Istanbul has some traffic rules of its own and it is important to know that before getting here. Although the traffic seems disorganized at first, you will soon start to perceive it as a both complex and chaotic dance, and strangely enough, everybody knows the steps. I rarely saw car accidents in Istanbul, and when I did they were minor. There is one important thing you should keep in mind though, their crosswalks are purely decorative and in Istanbul it's the pedestrians that are allowing cars to pass, not vice versa. Just to be safe, cross the street only when there's no car approaching.

5. KEEP CALM AND DRINK CAY

"Conversations without tea are like a night sky without the moon "– folk saying from Sivas Turkey

Turkish people are huge tea lovers. They will serve it anywhere, anytime and to anybody that will accept their invitation, as a sign of hospitality and friendship. Serving tea is profoundly inserted into the Turkish culture and it helps you better understand the customs and relations between locals.

All over Istanbul you can find the famous tea gardens called Çay Bahçesi. Many of them are located in areas with spectacular views over the Bosphorus so it's worth stopping over to try one of their many tea specialties and maybe even exchange some stories with the locals.

If you want something special, Café Loti is the place to go. Situated on a hill, with a bird's - eye view over the city, the café received its name after the famous French writer Pierre Loti, who used to come here often to admire the city from above. In the summer, the place gets very crowded and it's often hard to find a place.

6. SEAGULL'S EMPIRE

Together with the cats, seagulls are the second most popular non-human figures in Istanbul. Whenever you will take a cruise or cross the Bosphorus with the ferry you will see people buying two pretzels. One will be for them and one for feeding the seagulls. In fact, the seagulls of Istanbul are among the fattest ones I ever saw in my life and from what I noticed, they like swimming more than flying. They are also extremely photogenic and they will happily smile in all the pictures you will take with Bosphorus. They will also get angry and scream at you, but everybody is ignoring their crisis and accepts their tantrums the way you are forced to accept a family member with anger management issues.

7. IT'S FOOTBALL NOT SOCCER

Turkish men are passionate about football. So much that whenever there is a football game going on, the traffic gets blocked. With three big football clubs existing at the moment, be sure that there will be at least one game playing during the time that you

19

are visiting. If you are into football, don't worry, you will not lose the score. It will be everywhere on TV and there's no way to be avoided.

I even got married on a terrace overlooking Beşiktaş Stadium and I was "lucky" to have as accompanying music the loud cheers of the enthusiastic supporters. Half of my female guests had to climb the hill up to my wedding venue with shoes in their hands as all the roads were blocked by the people struggling to enter the stadium, and no car or taxi was allowed to pass by.

8. PRINCE ISLANDS

Don't be fooled by the name. You won't find any princes here except for the horses, although the islands received this name after being used as an exile destination for all the Byzantine disobeying princes and princesses. After the fall of Constantinople, the Ottomans kept the tradition by sending here those members of the Sultan's family who were falling in disgrace. Nowadays, the islands turned into a very popular tourist destination but also an exclusive and expensive location where some of the wealthiest families in Istanbul are owning holiday homes. The nine small islands that are forming Prince Islands are located in the Sea of Marmara, in the southeastern part of Istanbul. The biggest of them and the one I like the most is named Büyükada. You can reach it by ferry and the trip will take merely one hour. Among the two types of ferries departing from Kabataş you should choose the sea-busses which are faster. Weekends are usually very crowded but during the week days you'll be surprised by the serenity and holiday vibe that the islands have to offer. There are no cars on the islands, just bicycles and horse-drawn carriages. And if you want to experience great food with an incredible view I would recommend you to try Eskibağ Teras. One of Büyükada's best kept secret location, this dreamy place is set high up on a cliff, with breathtaking views of the sea and surrounded by Mediterranean vegetation. The service is friendly, the menu is diverse and the food is delicious.

9. IT'S NOT ALWAYS SUNNY IN ISTANBUL

As much as you envision Istanbul as a city blessed with perfect weather, mild winters and mostly sunny days, you'll be surprised to know that the weather here is like a bipolar capricious woman who will switch in a second from loving you warmly with all her heart, to simply ignoring you with coldness. Be sure to pack both light and warm clothes if you visit anytime between October and April and be prepared for many rainy days and snow in the winter. The best time to visit is spring and autumn, with summers being usually too hot and crowded, and winters too cold. If you'll organize your trip in April, May or September you'll experience a much friendlier and less capricious weather and you'll be able to enjoy more of the outdoor activities that the city has to offer, including a nice meal by the Bosphorus or a sunny boat tour of the city. And speaking of Bosphorus, this leads me to my next tip.

10. ON THE WAVES OF BOSPHORUS

"Life can't be all that bad,' I'd think from time to time. 'Whatever happens, I can always take a long walk along the Bosporus" – Orhan Pamuk.

Bosphorus is the core of Istanbul, a giant heart pumping restlessly its vital energy into the city's arteries. There are not too many locations in this world that had managed to impress me as much as seeing Bosphorus for the first time. This strategic waterway connecting the Black Sea to the Sea of Marmara is the source of power and rise of all the empires that, throughout the centuries, used to reside its shores. The name originates from the legend of Io, one of Zeus's lovers, and in Thracian language it meant "passage of the cow"- "When Hera, Zeus´ wife, suspected her husband being involved in a love affair with Io, Zeus converted Io in a small cow and tried to send her away from Hera´s rage. The cow swam across the strait but Hera discovered it and sent big flies after the cow to bite and disturb her, forcing Io to end up in the Aegean Sea (thus the name of Ionian Sea)".

The best part of Istanbul is located on the shores of Bosphorus, from the top hotels and restaurants to

23

beautiful villas and Ottoman palaces. In fact, the Bosphorus area, both the European and Asian sides, is considered to be one of the most expensive real estate markets in the world.

Not to be missed is a half day boat trip on the Bosphorus to admire both shores up to Anadolu Kavağı, a fishing village on the Asian side, where you can visit the ruins of Yoros Castle.

11. "BACK TO THE FUTURE"

If you are passionate about the psychic practices of future prediction, Istanbul is the right place for you. Fate reading from Turkish coffee is quite popular here and the city is home to many places where you may find the famous fortune tellers. They can see the future but only in Turkish so it's recommended that you take a local with you or somebody that understands the language. Just make sure that it's someone that has your best interest at heart and doesn't want to change your future.

12. NOT THE BEST PLACE FOR A RECOVERING SHOPAHOLIC

I love shopping. It's a sort of therapeutic practice for me and it's the only thing I found so far that can calm my wondering mind and keep it from continuously ruminating. But like any responsible grown up that I'm supposed to be, I am desperately trying to keep my shopping urges under control. Unfortunately, Istanbul makes my life so hard in this regard. With a multitude of malls, street shops or souks, you can find everything here, no matter if you are searching for something modern

The famous Grand Bazar, a must see in Istanbul even if you are not passionate about shopping, is one of the oldest and largest covert markets in the world, with a number of more than 3.000 shops under its roof. For sure not your average neighborhood shopping mall, the offer here is inexhaustible, but the most sought-after products are the jewelries, the carpets and the leather goods. The only things you need are money, good negotiation skills and patience to go through the many stores spread over the 60 streets which make up the market. Shopping is not the only thing that you can do in the Bazar. You can also find here many restaurants, cafes and even mosques.

If you're searching for a more exclusive shopping experience and you don't like crowded places, Istinye Park, Kanyon Mall or Zorlu Center are the destinations for you.

Another address not to be missed by any true shopaholic is the Nişantaşı district, an upper-scale residential and shopping area. Considered to be among the most expensive streets in Istanbul, you can find here both prestigious Turkish brands and world known luxury retail stores. To enjoy more of the upper-class atmosphere, grab a drink or a quick lunch at Brasserie Nişantaşı

13. RAKI ON

Rakı, Turkey's unofficial national drink, has more traditions than a royal family. There's a whole culture formed around this strong liquor and the beverage is popular around the whole country. There are many stories that Turkish people like to tell about rakı, but the one I found the most amusing and explanatory for why the drink is also called "Lion milk", is the story of the mouse experiment: "Four mice are locked in a cage and forced to taste four different types of alcohol. The first one tries wine and falls asleep.

Second one tries vodka and falls asleep. Third one tries whiskey and falls asleep. The forth one tries rakı and with a proud and strong voice gets on top of the cage and shouts: - Bring me the cat, there's something that I need to discuss with her".

Rakı is usually served as an appetizer, but the practice here is that once you'll finish the first glass, you will have it refilled continuously throughout the whole meal. You should always drink it cold, mixed with water and ice. And one more important thing... Never order just one glass for you because it's considered impolite here. Always order one bottle for the whole table as rakı is not the drink to have by yourself. It is best associated with great company, good conversations and a positive mood.

If you want to taste a glass of rakı sprinkled with a touch of local history you can try the 1924 Istanbul (Rejans) Restaurant. Mustafa Kemal Ataturk had a favorite table here and it's still reserved for him.

14. CURRENCY

Turkey's national currency is the Turkish Lira. Although almost everywhere in the touristic areas you can also pay with dollars and euros, it is more advantageous for you to keep your money in Turkish Liras. You can find ATMs almost everywhere throughout the city and when you withdraw money from your debit or credit card you have the option to do it in both local liras and foreign currencies (dollars or euros).

15. IN BED WITH AGATHA CHRISTIE

The hotel market in Istanbul is so rich and diverse that any type of traveler can find something for his or hers liking. According to your budget, you will encounter here a wide variety of choices from bed & breakfasts or house sharing to five-star luxury hotels.

Among the many places to choose among, there are some that have a special story to tell:

Pera Palace – Dating back to 1892, is the first western hotel built in Istanbul, originally for the use of the passengers of Orient Express train. A still functioning hotel nowadays, it can also be considered a museum due to the amount of famous people that passed its doors throughout the years, among them Agatha Christie, Ernest Hemingway and Mustafa Kemal Ataturk, the father of modern Turkey. If you want to sleep in Agatha Christie's bed you have the chance to do so by booking room 411. And if you are a writer, you may even catch some inspiration as rumors say that this was the room in which Agatha Christies completed her writings on the famous book Murder on The Orient Express.

Four Seasons Hotel Istanbul At Sultanahmet – located in the old and fascinating district of Sultanahmet, close to Hagia Sofia, this hotel was originally built in 1918 as an Ottoman murderer's prison. Closed in 1969, the building restarted activity in 1980 as a military prison and in 1996, after facing an intense restoration, opened its gates again as a four-star luxury hotel.

Çırağan Palace Kempinski Istanbul – standing proud on the shores of Bosphorus, this hotel has served as residence for several sultans and even hosted the seat of the Turkish Parliament. The most beautiful hotel in Istanbul from my point of view, with amazing views of the Bosphorus, gorgeous interiors and impeccable service.

16. MAKE A WISH

There's no doubt that Istanbul is a mystic city that can charm you and embrace you in a way that not many cities can. On top of its magic, the city hosts many locations that can make your biggest desires come true. Make sure you visit Telli Baba tomb if you wish to get married or Tuzbaba Türbesi, built in the honor of Sultan Mehmet's "Salt Master", a place famous for the many miracles it had fulfilled.

Eyüp Sultan Tomb is one of the most important destinations in Istanbul. People come here not only for praying at the Prophet's tomb but also for attaching colorful strings on the branches. The strings are symbols of their wishes that have been fulfilled.

One more stop on the map of wish fulfilling places is the Yahya Efendi Turbesi tomb. A famous mystic in the Ottoman Empire and milk brother to Suleiman the Magnificent, his tomb was built by one of the most talented architects during the Ottoman Empire, Mimar Sinan.

17. SALT UP YOUR LIFE

If you are a steak lover maybe you have already heard about the internet sensation Nusret Gökçe better known as Salt Bae. The founder of Nusr-Et restaurants with locations all over the world, rose to fame in Istanbul, where he opened his first restaurant in 2010. He gained world vide popularity with an online video of himself that went viral overnight.

If you want to taste his famous steak and see for yourself what the fuss is all about, you can try his newly opened restaurant in the Grand Bazar.

18. SUNDAY NOT SO FUN DAY

If you visit Istanbul over the weekend and you want to make the most out of your Sunday here than you need a proper plan of attack in order to maximize your time, avoid the huge crowds and the traffic jams. Especially if the weather is nice, the city will be packed, everybody will be out, eating, drinking tea, or visiting touristic sites. There will also be a great influx of people coming from the countryside to enjoy the city for the day. If you want to use this day to visit touristic objectives I advise you to do this early in the morning. The majority of them are opening at 8:30 so

31

the earliest you'll get there the most chances you'll have to not spend a long time in the ques. Also keep in mind that the Grand Bazar and the Spice Market are closed on Sundays.

What I would advise you to do is to reserve this day to visit the Asian side of Istanbul. Not so crowded with tourists and only a short ride away by ferry from the European side, if you visit the district of Üsküdar, you will have a better idea about how the locals live while still staying anchored in the city's history.

19. TRANSPORTATION

I have a confession to make. I am absolutely terrified of driving in Istanbul, although I've been driving all over the world for more than 15 years. On top of that, without false modesty, I really consider myself to be a good driver. But Istanbul traffic has always managed to petrify me. Based on my experience, I wouldn't recommend you to rent a car during your stay here. Driving in Istanbul will cause you nothing but stress and you'll end up being more preoccupied about how to drive and where to park instead of enjoying the city. For the airport transfer to your hotel you can take a taxi or an uber or you can arrange with your hotel to be picked up by a shuttle. Taxis are generally safe here, the only issue you can sometimes face is getting an extended trip. Turkish taxi drivers like to overcharge unsuspecting tourists but I guess this is pretty normal in any major city around the world. As some general rules, only use official yellow cabs with the logo and number of the company on the doors, and during your trip, if it's possible, use a GPS on your phone to see where the driver is taking you. While you're in Istanbul you can also hire a driver to take you around the city but my advice is that you shouldn't rely on this type of transportation too much. Traffic is jammed and slow especially during rush hour and you'll end up losing too much of a precious time. The fastest options are the subway and the tram lines. Try to book a hotel close to your area of interest and walk as much as possible. The colorful and diverse street life is part of Istanbul's charm and you'll be surprised by how many more details you'll be able to observe during your walks.

*"To savor Istanbul's back
streets, to appreciate the vines and
trees that endow its ruins with
accidental grace, you must, first
and foremost, be a stranger to
them."*

– Orhan Pamuk.

20. HOSPITALITY WAS BORN HERE

Local people of Istanbul are kind and friendly and they treat tourists with genuine care and respect. This comes from the fact that the people here really like foreigners. Whatever need or wish you'll have during your stay, there will always be somebody happy to help you, and the general feeling you'll get throughout your holiday will be that you are considered a very important guest here. Locals are very proud of their country and they'll gladly share stories with you while inviting you for a glass of cay.

Offering food, drinks and gifts to the tourists is a form of social expression for the people of Istanbul, but also a way of sharing their cultural identity.

Since living in Istanbul, I began to get used with Turkish people's way of social interaction and I'm trying to respect their culture and customs as much as possible. Although I am obsessed with punctuality, I learned that here people are not criticized for being late and even in business meetings everybody is very relaxed, never in a hurry and serious matters are always discussed after having tea and some small talk. I also learned to always have consideration towards everybody around me and never eat or drink something without offering to share it with the others.

21. READY, SET, ACTION!

Istanbul is the perfect set for shooting a movie. The city's oriental characteristics mixed with European attitudes make it a unique location that even Hollywood fell in love with. For a long time, filmmakers from all over the world have been flocking to Istanbul, trying to make the most out of the city's most iconic locations. Many famous blockbusters were shot here, including three of the James Bond movies, The World is not enough, From Russia with love and Skyfall. If you are a James Bond fan and you want to see some of the locations that were used during the shootings you will find them in Grand Bazar, Eminonu Square, the New Mosque, Hagia Sophia, Galata Bridge and Basilica Cistern, just to name a few.

The Turkish TV series industry is not very old but managed to reach a boom during the last twenty years becoming world-wide famous and intensely promoting Turkey's image on an international scale. Having 6 different series each night on TV, you can run into celebrities anywhere while walking around the city. If you like series and you want to try a Turkish one based on historical facts and local figures I would strongly recommend Suleiman the Magnificent. This ambitious historical production is based on real events that took place on the territory of the Ottoman Empire during the 19th century and portrays the life and reign of Suleiman I, the tenth sultan of the Ottoman Empire.

22. THE IST FACTOR

We like to call it the Ist Factor here and there's no shortage of them. Music is one of the key ingredients that form the Turkish daily life and legacy. There is even a legend that locals like to tell about how music was born in Turkey –" One day, while returning home from hunting, a young man heard a very beautiful and distinct sound. Trying to see where the sound was coming from he spotted a horse skull. Several hair shafts were wrapped around the skull vibrating from the wind. The hunter took the skull and tried to mimic the sounds, batting the pace with his fingers. He managed to reproduce the beautiful sounds and that is how the first-string instrument was born."

Much like all the aspects of Turkish culture, music is also a mix of styles and historical influences. Turkish traditional music is composed of elements from the Greek Orthodox Church and Byzantine secular music to which Jewish, Greek, Armenian and Turkish influences were added during the Ottoman period. One of the oldest types of music from Istanbul dates back to the Byzantine times of Constantinople, with byzantine legacy still being very well preserved in Turkey even today. During the Ottoman Empire, a large and distinct number of non-Muslim populations moved to Constantinople from different regions of the world, bringing with them their own language, instruments and diverse types of music. With such a rich legacy behind it's no wonder that the today's Turkish music is so diverse.

23. HAMMAM TO BE

No trip to Istanbul will be complete unless you'll visit a traditional Turkish bath called hammam. In order to truly understand Istanbul's history, you will also need to understand the concept of hammam. Hammams can be considered the essence of Turkish lifestyle throughout the times. In the local culture, cleanliness is assumed to be an attribute of divinity and that is why many hammams were built close to the mosques.

Architecturally speaking, most hammams are built the same way, with a marble podium placed in the middle and covered by a huge central dome, with small windows carved in the surrounding walls to allow the natural light to enter. In all hammams you will find a room where you can have a foam bath or a massage, a hot room where you'll be washed and a cold room to relax and have a cup of tea. This room is called "camekan" in Turkish.

A funny tradition related to hammams and one that my husband "threatened" me with before we got married, was that in Turkey, the mother of the boy has to take her future daughter in law to hammam and thoroughly inspect her body before marriage. If she is to find anything strange, unusual or inappropriate she is supposed to inform her son. I found out later from my amused mother in law that this practice dated back to the old times and is no longer common today.

There are many hammams that you can try throughout Istanbul but if you want a special experience don t go to the ones located inside hotels and try a real traditional one like Kilic Ali Paşa Hamam or Kadirga Hamam.

24. THE ART OF BARGAINING

In case you didn't 'know, bargaining is a practice that can be brought to a state of art and you can learn that quite fast, in just a few days' stay in Istanbul. On my first visit here, I was told that if you don't bargain in Grand Bazar you will be considered rude by the merchants. And although I was not too much accustomed with bargaining and I was quite ashamed to do it in the beginning, I managed to understand its mechanism and even get a glimpse of the pleasure that both the seller and the buyer can feel after a good bargain. You just need to be firm and show no sign of emotion because Turkish people are great merchants and negotiators and they will instantly detect any sign that you are pulling back. When you want to buy something here, especially in the Grand Bazar and Spice Market, never agree to pay the price that is displayed. After a bit of insisting, the merchants will usually tell you that they will make a special price for you. If you get a good offer, buy more products from the same seller. The more you'll buy from the same place the better price you'll get. And since the majority of merchants are men, if you'll start a small discussion about football you'll definitely get an even better deal.

25. SPICES OF THE WORLD

Hello Spice Market! Get ready to enrich your senses with the flavors of the Orient and delight your eyes with a feast of colors. Dating back to 1664, The Spice Market or Egyptian Bazar, is the second largest market in Istanbul after the Grand Bazar and home to dozens of types of spices, different varieties of sweets, teas and honey. Another delicacy that you may find here is the rarest and most expensive form of caviar, the Iranian caviar. I would recommend you to make a list of what you want to buy because, if you are anything like me, you will be so confused by the huge selection you'll see in the market that you'll end up buying nothing from what you had initially planned. And one last piece of advice, don't buy the spices from inside the Market as they are more expensive. The locals are usually buying everything from the streets running behind the Bazar.

26. GET WELL SOON

If you're afraid you might get sick during your vacation, worry no more. Turkish health system is among the best ones in the world and Istanbul private hospitals look like 5-star luxury hotels. In fact, there are many countries who are sending their patients here, through medical tourism agencies, because Turkey managed to reach the level of Germany or Austria in terms of medical care, but with lower prices. Health safety should always be considered when visiting a new place, especially if you are traveling with your kids.

27. MAIDEN'S TOWER

Located on the Asian side in the Uskudar district, the Maiden Tower also called Kız Kulesi in Turkish, is a place that has always fascinated me not only with the feeling of loneliness and isolation it projects but also because of the many legends related to it. The one I like the most says that: "Long time ago, a byzantine king built this place to protect his daughter from all the dangers that could threaten her life. When she was young, the fortunetellers predicted that she will die at a young age, bitten by a snake. One day, a servant brought the princess a basket full of apples unaware that a serpent was hiding inside. The snake jumped out and bit the princess and thus fulfilled the prophecy regarding her destiny".

Dating back to 1110, the Tower has been used for a variety of purposes among them as lighthouse during Ottoman times, while in 1829, it became a refugee location from the cholera epidemic. Later on, it also served as transit point for the state members that were sent in exile or who were supposed to be executed.

The World Is Not enough movie with James Bond was shot here in 1998, this being also the year that the Tower got its last restoration.

The interior has been since converted into an upscale restaurant, where you can enjoy a great lunch or dinner while admiring the city. And if you're looking for a unique wedding venue you should take the Maiden Tower into consideration.

28. FISHERMEN OF GALATA BRIDGE

Whenever I think about Galata Bridge the image that instantly comes to my mind is the portrait of the hundreds of fishermen holding their tackles up in the air. With a clear view towards Asia on the East and Europe on the West, the bridge is emblematic for the vibrant energy of Istanbul. Galata Bridge is my favorite spot for people watching. Locals smoking nargile and eating pretzels, tourists running around and taking pictures, or fishermen in action, you will find them all here in the same place. The fishermen spend sometimes the whole day on the bridge and it's not only for catching fish but also for the pleasure of social interaction with each other or with the tourists.

While here, you must try the hot corn on the cob, the pretzels or the fish sandwiches sold around the bridge. They are cheap and tasty and a good choice for a quick bite on the run.

29.FLYING FROM GALATA TOWER

After crossing the Galata Bridge, you should continue your walk towards Galata Tower. There' s a local legend saying that the first man that flew with the help of a pair of improvised wings, was a Greek living in Constantinople in the 17th century. Supposedly, he jumped from Galata Tower, crossed Bosporus and landed in Uskudar. Weather this story is real or not it couldn't be proved, but it's worth going to the tower and try to draw some conclusions by yourself. The place is very narrow inside and climbing the spiraled wooden stairs up to the top terrace will be quite difficult especially if you have a bit of claustrophobia. If you don't like climbing stairs you can opt for the easy way out and use the elevator taking you to the restaurant on top. Just a few stairs away from the rounded terrace with the panoramic view of the city, the restaurant gives you the chance to recharge your batteries with a glass of cay or a tasty meal before continuing with your tour.

30. RUSSIAN PERFUME

Reserve one evening to have dinner inside Çiçek Pasajı (The Flower Pasaj) originally called the Cité de Péra. This beautiful location was home away from home for many Russian families who found refugee here during the 1917 Russian emigration, leaving their country in order to escape the Bolshevik persecution. Among them, there were intellectuals, businessmen but also army officers or members of the Russian Imperial Government. In order to survive, without any money or housing, many of them started to sell flowers and around the 1940s, the biggest part of the building was occupied by their flower shops, hence the name Flower Pasaj. After the restoration in 1988, the Pasaj reopened as a gallery of pubs and restaurants, while still preserving its original decorations and architectural charm.

31. SUNSET WITH DESCARTES

Sunsets in Istanbul are magnificent and if you want to have front row to the show you should find a seat on top of Çamlıca Hill. Located on the Asian side, the highest hill in Istanbul and the place from where you can see all Istanbul from above, is a quiet escape from the city's constant buzz. Asked about the last place he would want to see before dying, the famous Renee Descartes chose Çamlıca Hill. Once you'll visit you will understand why.

32. WHISPERS OF THE HAREM

Even before arriving in Istanbul for the first time, I knew I wanted to visit Topkapi Palace. I have always been fascinated by the opulent lives of sultans and how their daily life was unfolding inside the palace, but most of all I was eager to know more about the mysterious existence of the women behind the harem's walls. For almost 400 years, Topkapi palace was the administrative, educational and artistic center of the Ottoman Empire, its mind and heart, but also the residence of the sultans. Today, you can visit and admire it in all its lost glory thanks to 50 years of intense restorations. Being one of the most visited places in Istanbul it is always crowded with tourists so try to organize your visit early in the morning and start with the Harem museum, as it is one of the most popular parts and it usually becomes the busiest.

The Harem initially had another location, but during the reign of Sultan Murad III, a few additional buildings were added to the Palace and the Harem moved here. Meaning "forbidden" in Arabic, the access inside the Harem was completely restricted for strangers, thus the birth of many stories and legends surrounding the chambers and the women inside them. The Harem family was occupying around 300 rooms and was composed of the wives, concubines and children of the Sultan, all of them guarded by black eunuchs and ruled by the Queen mother. The mother of the Sultan had the highest hierarchy inside the Harem but she also had a great influence regarding the affairs of the empire.

The concubines were chosen among the most beautiful and healthy women of different nationalities and different parts of the world. Some of them were caught as slaves, some were brought to the Palace as gifts for the Sultan while others were sent here by their families in hope of a better life. The majority of girls were brought to the Palace at a very young age and raised under strict discipline, and most of them were growing up with the hope to catch the sultan's attention and have a chance to become consorts or sometimes even wives. Among all the women of the Harem, there is one in particular that changed history.

The Russian slave Roxelana, thanks to her scheming, ambition and cruelty, managed to become the favorite wife of Suleiman the Magnificent and to actually rule the Ottoman Empire from behind the curtains. She was the only woman to gain so much power while coming from such a humble background. Two of her sons, Mehmet and Selim, followed Suleiman to the throne and became sultans of the Ottoman Empire.

All these stories are dust of the past now but the locals say that sometimes, if you listen carefully, you can still hear the cries and wails of the thousands of women who lived between these walls.

33. TURKISH PAPER MARBLING

Istanbul is not only a sightseeing destination but a place where you can also learn something new in the local tradition. You may find here a special type of art that can awaken your hidden talents and create some incredible results while the best part is that it is impossible to do it wrong. Paper marbling or Ebru, is a very strange form of painting that is produced by using dyes, a solution based of water and special tools, with a finished result that is similar to marble patterns. There are many places throughout Istanbul where you can learn about the history of Ebru, how to prepare the dyes and the special liquid, how to make Ebru brushes and in the end, create your own piece of art.

For workshops, you can book a class at Les Arts Turcs - Art Gallery & Studio in the Sultanahmet district.

34. MINIATURK PARK

Don't panic that you won't have enough time to visit everything that you had planned during your stay in Istanbul. You just need to visit Miniaturk Park to see it all. If you are travelling with your kids, this will be a place they will enjoy also.

Miniaturk park museum is a small replica of a big world. You will find here mini representations of the main Istanbul touristic sights but also attractions from Anatolia or the Ottoman territories from outside of Turkey. Basically, in just one place, you will find all the major touristic attractions the country has to offer. Covering an area of 60 000 square meters, Miniaturk Park is considered to be the biggest miniature park in the world.

35. SOME GUILTY PLEASURES

Among the many types of Turkish specialties, there's one that I have a soft spot for - the goat milk ice cream. I don't even like ice-cream in general but this one is something special. Turkish ice cream has in interesting story. It is called dondurma and if you walk the streets of Istanbul you will find many vendors that will amaze you with their skills of stretching the ice cream so much that it will look like long mozzarella strands. This transformation is possible because the ice cream here has an elastic and gummy structure given by the use of salep, a powdered ingredient obtained from the bulbs of a certain type of orchid, and mastic, a resin secreted by the mastic tree. The ice-cream can be so dense sometimes that you can even eat with a knife and fork.

If you love ice-cream you must put this one on your bucket list.

36. TRY THE NARGILE

On the shores of Bosphorus, there's a nice place called Huqqa where me and my husband like to go sometimes and enjoy a nargile.

People have been enjoying nargile (Turkish Water Pipe) for hundreds of years and this tradition dates back to 1500s in the Middle East. Around the sixteenth century, nargile made its way to the Ottoman Empire and tobacco smoking through the hookah quickly became a symbol of social status. There are many paintings illustrating high-ranked dignitaries and sultans smoking nargile and in those times, smoking with the sultan was considered the highest honor you could receive. Most of the pipes were made of wood and various metals and Turkish craftsmen were using them to demonstrate their artistic and decorative techniques.

Today smoking nargile is a common practice throughout the whole Turkey, with a large variety of flavors to choose among. There are many ways to savor them but my favorite one is prepared with a milk base and with melon flavored tobacco. Just take care, nargiles are very strong and should not be smoked often as one puff is the equivalent to smoking 10 cigarettes.

37. TAKE ME TO THE BEACH

Among the best parts of living in Istanbul is that whenever you want to enjoy a day of beach, sea, sun and chill you can do it by just jumping in your car and driving for 45 minutes. It is all just around the corner, on one of the many beaches surrounding the city. With Marmara Sea in the south and Black Sea in the north there's plenty of options to choose among. My favorite one… True Blue Beach. On the shores of Black Sea, this beach is the perfect spot to admire the sea and the boats departing from the marina. Spend there the whole day and wait for the sunset. You won't be disappointed. Don't forget to bring along some beach towels, umbrellas and good mood, and if you're lucky enough you may even catch a live music concert.

38. KEYIF – THE ART OF RELAXATION

The Turkish practice of kef could be translated as a pleasurable state of relaxation and well-being, an elaborate art of doing absolutely nothing. For the people of Istanbul, it's a secret weapon to deal with the city's constant restlessness and it's an integral part of the day-to-day life. Keyif teaches you to find the joy of simple and pleasant things while trying to get rid of any stressful preoccupations. The locals here will teach you how important it is to devote a small part of each day to doing some pleasant activities while emptying our minds of unnecessary worries. You can practice keyif by listening to music, stretching your body or smoking nargile the only condition being that you have to be fully anchored in the moment and in what you are doing, without allowing your mind to wonder.

39. WHAT YOU SEE IS NOT ALWAYS WHAT YOU GET

With a city as complex and mysterious as Istanbul, there's no wonder that there is much more to discover than the obvious that meets the eye. Hidden below the surface, you can find a multitude of underground structures, tunnels and passages which were used in the past for storing and supplying water.

Basilica Cistern, originally named Yerebatan Sarayi or the Sunken Palace because of its dramatic 336 marble columns rising from the water, is one of the most famous wonders of Istanbul's underground.

Resembling more to a temple than a cistern, the name of this underground structure comes from a large public square located on the First Hill of Constantinople, named Basilica Stoa, under which the cistern was built. The ancient texts state that 7 000 slaves worked to build this tank which provided water for the Great Palace of Constantinople and to some of the surrounding establishments located on the First Hill. The cistern continued its mission of serving water even after the Ottoman conquest in 1453.

There are many interesting stories about Istanbul's secret underworld and some of the most captivating ones are related to the tunnels underneath Hagia Sofia, which are supposedly forming a sort of a spider web crossing a big part of the city's underground. Although the structure has been investigated by researchers since the middle of the 1900's, there is still little known about what really lies underneath there. Some legends state that the tunnels are wide enough to allow ships to pass through them and that they were built to provide a pathway from Topkapi Palace to Princess Islands.

40. THE CITY THAT NEVER SLEEPS

Istanbul at night is pure eye-candy! It is one of those types of cities that manages to metamorphosis itself into a completely different being when the night falls. Under the spell of dark everything looks more flattering, the streets are less crowded, terraces are full of tourists and the play between light and dark makes the sights look even more spectacular. The entertainment offer is incredibly diverse, ranging from stylish roof top terraces to cozy jazz bars, and from traditional Turkish pubs to luxurious nightclubs.

With nightlife centers like Ortaköy by the Bosphorus, Istiklal Street and Beşiktaş district, Istanbul is an incredibly cool city, among the coolest ones in Europe from my opinion. The bars and restaurants are packed each night and the locals will be more than happy to teach you how to choose the best locations according to quality of service, products served and interior decorations. It's not only the new modern places that attract the visitors but also the traditional Turkish taverns, soaked with the flavor of Istanbul and the perfume of the times that had passed.

Beyoğlu is the core of the city's night life. The bars and restaurants here are open each night all year long but their most popular time is during the summer months. Many of them have open-air terraces and rooftops where you can attend concerts or festivals while admiring unique views of the Bosphorus.

41. HAGIA SOPHIA – THE MOST BEAUTIFUL CHURCH IN THE WORLD

An absolute must see if you visit Istanbul! There are so many mysteries and legends related to Hagia Sophia that one book would not be enough to contain them all.

Considered the most beautiful church in the world, it was originally built as an orthodox church by the Byzantine king Justinian I. In 1453 during Mehmed II's conquer of Istanbul the church was transformed into a mosque and in 1934, at the wish of Mustafa Kemal Ataturk, first president of Turkey, it became a museum. One of the many legends surrounding this magnificent construction refers to the "disappearing of Constantine, the last emperor of Constantinople. His body was never found after the conquest of the city so the legend grew that he would one day return and, entering the Hagia Sophia by the imperial entrance, would turn the building back into being a church".

What is interesting is that in 2009, a group of archeology professors at the University of Istanbul discovered hidden entries that led to two existing tunnels in the basement of the Church. Until now, archeologists have found a number of tunnels and a few rooms but the largest underground part is still unknown.

Hagia Sophia or the church of "Holy Wisdom" is a monument of architectural courage that could not be equaled for a millennium. There is always a queue at the entrance to the Church but don't let it scare you. It usually moves fast and once you'll enter prepare to be overwhelmed by the beauty and grandeur of the dome of Saint Sofia, with its already famous golden mosaics.

42. PICNICKING

In Istanbul, we love to eat outdoors. As soon as the spring comes you will see many people having picnic throughout the city. Almost any green space can be used as a picnic place but usually the parks and areas around Bosporus are the most sought for. Usually people prepare for picnic by cooking in the house and the most common foods served are koftes, boreks, deserts and fruits. Don't worry about improvising. Just grab a blanket, a basket with some goodies and a pot of tea and head out to enjoy your very own local picnic.

43. WHIRLING TO INFINITY

Among the many fabulous, almost sacred spaces built throughout Istanbul, you may find some which host displays of a mystical ancient performance: The Whirling Dervishes Dance. Dating back to 1312 and with origins in Sufism and the Mevlevi Order, this mesmerizing spinning meditation is nowadays offered to us as a cultural event, organized by the Ministry of Culture and Tourism.

If you wish to take part in this amazing spectacle then prepare to let yourself entranced by the sound of the sacred music and by the whirling, celestial movement of the mystic dancers. They continuously rotate around themselves, as the planets do around their axis, and all together around the stars, keeping the Universe alive with their eternal vibration and ascending rotation, higher and higher...And for a second in a lifetime, and like a sparkle of light in Eternity, together with them, you might feel closer to God.

Best places to watch them: Galata Mevlevihanesi, Sirkeci Train Station and Hodjapasha.

44. THE ART SCENE

Istanbul has become during the recent years a big player in the global art world and this is just a normal route for a city so rich in history, cultural and ethnic influences. With a constant flow of inspiration and creativity streaming from every corner, there is also a constant grow of art galleries, programs in universities and festivals for supporting new artists.

If you visit Istanbul and you want to taste a bit of the local art flavor I could recommend you a few of my favorite local museums and art galleries.

Pera Museum – opened in 2005, the Museum exhibits in a chronological order the rich cultural heritage of Istanbul having three permanent exhibitions that you can visit: "Oriental paintings", "Anatolian measures and weights" and "Kutahya mosaic and ceramics". The museum also hosts exhibitions of international famous artists like Picasso, Rembrandt or Kahlo.

Salt – if you want to learn more about the architectural and economical history of the city or simply admire exhibitions of international famous artists, you can visit the two Salt institutions. Located one in Beyoglu and the other in Galata the institutions have a research center, a walk-in cinema a book store and a large space designated for exhibitions. The entry is free.

Sakıp Sabancı Museum – my favorite museum in Istanbul with an amazing location on the Bosporus, was opened to public in 2002 by Sakip Sabanci, a Turkish business man and member of one of the richest families in Turkey. The museum hosts a permanent collection of manuscripts, books, rare editions of the Koran, prayer books, imperial decrees and calligraphy instruments.

Most art galleries are located in Beyoglu and if you want to visit some I would recommend you Pilot Gallery, Galerist and Arter.

45. THE MANY MOSQUES

Istanbul hosts many mosques, 3000 to be more exact. Among this colossal number which can be quite overwhelming when you visit Istanbul for the first time, there is one in particular which impressed me the most: The Blue Mosque – this Turkish architectural masterpiece was built around 1609, during the reign of Ahmed I. Like many other mosques, this one also hosts the grave of its founder and is still used for religious purposes. The name comes from the 21.000 blue ceramic tiles brought from Iznic (Niceea) which were used for the interior decorations. The Blue Mosque is the only Mosque with 6 minarets in Turkey while the others have a maximum of 4. One of the legends regarding the construction of the mosque states that the construction "was the result of a misunderstanding between the sultan and his architect. The sultan supposedly had asked to have altın minare (minarets in gold) and the architect understood altı minare (which means six minarets). "

Suleymaniye (the Magnificent) – is the second most important mosque that I would strongly recommend you to visit during your stay here. Immersing from the old center of Istanbul and overlooking the Golden Horn, close to the Egyptian Bazar, Suleiman's Mosque is one of the most important Muslim buildings throughout the whole Turkey. Among the biggest mosques in the city, the edifice was built by the famous architect Sinan, during Istanbul's most glorious period under the reign of Sultan Suleiman the Magnificent. After 30 years of being in power, the Sultan wanted to build something unique as a symbol of his reign. Suleiman's mosque is undoubtedly one of the greatest architectural successes and is considered to be the most beautiful imperial mosque in Istanbul.

Important to know before your visit is that tourist visits inside the mosques are forbidden during prayers, which take place five times a day. Please respect the local culture and don't dress in shorts or skirts when planning to visit a mosque and cover your head and shoulders if you are a woman. Leave your shoes at the entrance and try to not bother the others by being too loud or using your cell phone.

46. ALWAYS A KID AT HEART

Istanbul Toy Museum is the place to go when you want to make your inner child happy. As a kid who loved her toys and had unique names designated for each and every one of them, discovering this place gave me a lot of joy. Among so many places burdened by the weight and severity of the past, this museum is a sweet escape to the land of no worries. Located on the Asian side and built inside a traditional wooden house dating back to the 1800s the museum was created by the famous writer and poet Sunay Akın, whose collection of 4 000 toys gathered from all over the world has been displayed throughout the four floors of the building. Prepare for a feeling of both amazement and nostalgia while admiring the many different types of doll houses, fabulous puppets, musical instruments and space crafts.

47. DOLMABAHCE PALACE

Also named Versailles of the East, Dolmabahce Palace is an amazing and opulent construction which resembles more to an Austrian or French Imperial Palace than to an oriental Residence. Decorated with elements of Baroc, Rococo and Neoclassic the palace was designated to have a functionality that preserved the Ottoman tradition. Built during the 19th century, Dolmabahce is probably one of the most complete palace museum in the world. Fourteen tons of gold in the form of foil were used to decorate the ceilings and the largest collection in the world of Baccarat and Bohemia crystal chandeliers can be admired throughout the rooms.

Surrounded by lush and perfectly manicured gardens and with an amazing view of the Bosporus, the palace is also the largest one in Turkey with a surface of 45.000 square meters and 300 rooms. The Turkish people's admiration and care for this place grew considerably since Mustafa Kemal Ataturk, the father of modern Turkey, moved his residence here. Moreover, he died inside the palace and his room, kept intact, is one of the highlights of the touristic tours.

48. MUSEUM OF INNOCENCE

Turkey has some amazingly talented writers which is no wonder since being born in a country so rich in tradition, history and culture can make you nothing but creative. Among them, the Nobel awarded Orhan Pamuk is a favorite of mine.

Museum of Innocence was opened in Istanbul by Orhan Pamuk as a completion of his famous book with the same name. The museum hosts objects that Pamuk has bought from different antique fairs in Istanbul throughout the years.

Pamuk didn't get the idea of opening the museum after writing the book. He was passionate about antiques for long time and he was collecting them in parallel with his writing. The objects he was finding were becoming real characters in the book so it can be said that both the book and the museum came to life in the same time and grew together. The museum is located in Beyoglu, in a house which was representative for a middle-class family living in Istanbul in the 1970s, a society which claimed to be modern but whose roots were still strongly anchored in traditions.

The museum was awarded and designated as the European Museum of the Year in 2014.

49. HIPPODROME

Go visit the hippodrome for a glimpse inside the social life of the people during the Byzantine times.

One of the city's emblematic buildings, the At Meydani Hippodrome was initially the center of the public life, a space where all the sports and social activities where taking place. Today it is named Sultan Ahmet Market and only a few fragments of the original construction can be still admired. The horse races and gladiator games were great entertainment in Greek cities and also during the Roman and Byzantine times but all it is left of them today are memories of the past and fascinating stories to listen to.

50. RAHMI ÇOK MUSEUM

This museum is very interesting for everybody no matter the age. With a large collection of antique cars, steam engines, horse carriages, ships and submarines, be prepared to spend at least 4 hours here if you want to see them all. If you travel with your kids this place is a must see for them. You can even find a restaurant inside if you want to enjoy a quick lunch.

TOP REASONS TO BOOK THIS TRIP

" That was the moment when I
suddenly understood why and how
people could fall in love with
Istanbul, despite the immense pain
that this love was provoking them.
It was not easy to stop loving a city
so heartbreakingly beautiful "

– Elif Shafak

People – The people of Istanbul are among the friendliest and worm-hearted that I have ever met. You will instantly feel welcomed and treated like a family member.

Food - The food alone is a reason good enough to visit Istanbul. Diverse, unique, tasty, come to Istanbul to try Turkish gastronomy at its finest.

Historical Sights - With such an immense historical heritage, Istanbul is the most complex history class you'll ever have.

Diversity – From day to night and from one shore to the other Istanbul can offer you a complete holiday. Other Resources:

MAP OF ISTANBUL

https://istanbulmap360.com/istanbul-tourist-map#.XB5XeMaB2EI

BONUS BOOK

50 THINGS TO KNOW ABOUT PACKING LIGHT FOR TRAVEL

PACK THE RIGHT WAY EVERY TIME

AUTHOR: MANIDIPA BHATTACHARYYA

Edited by Melanie Howthorne

ABOUT THE AUTHOR

Manidipa Bhattacharyya is a creative writer and editor, with an
education in English literature and Linguistics. After working in the IT
industry for seven long years she decided to call it quits and follow her
heart instead. Manidipa has been ghost writing, editing, proof reading
and doing secondary research services for many story tellers and article
writers for about three years. She stays in Kolkata, India with her
husband and a busy two year old. In her own time Manidipa enjoys
travelling, photography and writing flash fiction.

Manidipa believes in travelling light and never carries anything that she
couldn't haul herself on a trip. However, travelling with her child
changed the scenario. She seemed to carry the entire world with her for
the baby on the first two trips. But good sense prevailed and she is
again working her way to becoming a light traveler, this time with a
kid.

INTRODUCTION

He who would travel happily
must travel light.

-Antoine de Saint-Exupéry

Travel takes you to different places from seas and mountains to deserts and much more. In your travels you get to interact with different people and their cultures. You will, however, enjoy the sights and interact positively with these new people even more, if you are travelling light.

When you travel light your mind can be free from worry about your belongings. You do not have to spend precious vacation time waiting for your luggage to arrive after a long flight. There is be no chance of your bags going missing and the best part is that you need not pay a fee for checked baggage.

People who have mastered this art of packing light will root for you to take only one carry-on, wherever you go. However, many people can find it really hard to pack light. More so if you are travelling with children. Differentiating between "must have" and "just in case" items is the starting point. There will be ample shopping avenues at your destination which are just waiting to be explored.

This book will show you 'packing' in a new 'light' – pun intended – and help you to embrace light packing practices for all of your future travels.

Off to packing!

DEDICATION

I dedicate this book to all the travel buffs that I know, who have given me great insights into the contents of their backpacks.

THE RIGHT TRAVEL GEAR

1. CHOOSE YOUR TRAVEL GEAR CAREFULLY

While selecting your travel gear, pick items that are light weight, durable and most importantly, easy to carry. There are cases with wheels so you can drag them along – these are usually on the heavy side because of the trolley. Alternatively a backpack that you can carry comfortably on your back, or even a duffel bag that you can carry easily by hand or sling across your body are also great options. Whatever you choose, one thing to keep in mind is that the luggage itself should not weigh a ton, this will give you the flexibility to bring along one extra pair of shoes if you so desire.

2. CARRY THE MINIMUM NUMBER OF BAGS

Selecting light weight luggage is not everything. You need to restrict the number of bags you carry as well. One carry-on size bag is ideal for light travel. Most carriers allow one cabin baggage plus one purse, handbag or camera bag as long as it slides under the seat in front. So technically, you can carry two items of luggage without checking them in.

3. PACK ONE EXTRA BAG

Always pack one extra empty bag along with your essential items. This could be a very light weight duffel bag or even a sturdy tote bag which takes up minimal space. In the event that you end up buying a lot of souvenirs, you already have a handy bag to stuff all that into and do not have to spend time hunting for an appropriate bag.

I'm very strict with my packing and have everything in its right place. I never change a rule. I hardly use anything in the hotel room. I wheel my own wardrobe in and that's it.

Charlie Watts

CLOTHES & ACCESSORIES

4. PLAN AHEAD

Figure out in advance what you plan to do on your trip. That will help you to pick that one dress you need for the occasion. If you are going to attend a wedding then you have to carry formal wear. If not, you can ditch the gown for something lighter that will be comfortable during long walks or on the beach.

5. WEAR THAT JACKET

Remember that wearing items will not add extra luggage for your air travel. So wear that bulky jacket that you plan to carry for your trip. This saves space and can also help keep you warm during the chilly flight.

6. MIX AND MATCH

Carry clothes that can be interchangeably used to reinvent your look. Find one top that goes well with a couple of pairs of pants or skirts. Use tops, shirts and jackets wisely along with other accessories like a scarf or a stole to create a new look.

7. CHOOSE YOUR FABRIC WISELY

Stuffing clothes in cramped bags definitely takes its toll which results in wrinkles. It is best to carry wrinkle free, synthetic clothes or merino tops. This will eliminate the need for that small iron you usually bring along.

8. DITCH CLOTHES PACK UNDERWEAR

Pack more underwear and socks. These are the things that will give you a fresh feel even if you do not get a chance to wear fresh clothes. Moreover these are easy to wash and can be dried inside the hotel room itself.

9. CHOOSE DARK OVER LIGHT

While picking your clothes choose dark coloured ones. They are easy to colour coordinate and can last longer before needing a wash. Accidental food spills and dirt from the road are less visible on darker clothes.

10. WEAR YOUR JEANS

Take only one pair of Jeans with you, which you should wear on the flight. Remember to pick a pair that can be worn for sightseeing trips and is equally eloquent for dinner. You can add variety by adding light weight cargoes and chinos.

11. CARRY SMART ACCESSORIES

The right accessory can give you a fresh look even with the same old dress. An intelligent neck-piece, a couple of bright scarves, stoles or a sarong can be used in a number of ways to add variety to your clothing. These light weight beauties can double up as a nursing cover, a light blanket, beach wear, a modesty cover for visiting places of worship, and also makes for an enthralling game of peek-a-boo.

12. LEARN TO FOLD YOUR GARMENTS

Seasoned travellers all swear by rolling their clothes for compact and wrinkle free packing. Bundle packing, where you roll the clothes around a central object as if tying it up, is also a popular method of compact and wrinkle free packing. Stacking folded clothes one on top of another is a big no-no as it makes creases extreme and they are difficult to get rid of without ironing.

13. WASH YOUR DIRTY LAUNDRY

One of the ways to avoid carrying loads of clothes is to wash the clothes you carry. At some places you might get to use the laundry services or a Laundromat but if you are in a pinch, best solution is to wash them yourself. If that is the plan then carrying quick drying clothes is highly recommended, which most often also happen to be the wrinkle free variety.

14. LEAVE THOSE TOWELS BEHIND

Regular towels take up a lot of space, are heavy and take ages to dry out. If you are staying at hotels they will provide you with towels anyway. If you are travelling to a remote place, where the availability of towels look doubtful, carry a light weight travel towel of viscose material to do the job.

15. USE A COMPRESSION BAG

Compression bags are getting lots of recommendation now days from regular travellers. These are useful for saving space in your luggage when you have to pack bulky dresses. While packing for the return trip, get help from the hotel staff to arrange a vacuum cleaner.

FOOTWEAR

16. PUT ON YOUR HIKING BOOTS

If you have plans to go hiking or trekking during your trip, you will need those bulky hiking boots. The best way to carry them is to wear them on flight to save space and luggage weight. You can remove the boots once inside and be comfortable in your socks.

17. PICKING THE RIGHT SHOES

Shoes are often the bulkiest items, along with being the dainty if you are a female. They need care and take up a lot of space in your luggage. It is advisable therefore to pick shoes very carefully. If you plan to do a lot of walking and site seeing, then wearing a pair of comfortable walking shoes are a must. For more formal occasions you can carry durable, light weight flats which will not take up much space.

18. STUFF SHOES

If you happen to pack a pair of shoes, ensure you utilize their hollow insides. Tuck small items like rolled up socks or belts to save space. They will also be easy to find.

TOILETRIES

19. STASHING TOILETRIES

Carry only absolute necessities. Airline rules dictate
that for one carry-on bag, liquids and gels must be in
3.4 ounce (100ml) bottles or less, and must be packed
in a one quart zip-lock bag. If you are planning to stay
in a hotel, the basic things will be provided for you.
It's best is to buy the rest from the local market at
your destination.

20. TAKE ALONG TAMPONS

Tampons are a hard to find item in a lot of countries.
Figure out how many you need and pack accordingly.
For longer stays you can buy them online and have
them delivered to where you are staying.

21. GET PAMPERED BEFORE YOU TRAVEL

Some avid travellers suggest getting a pedicure and
manicure just the day before travelling. This not only
gives you a well kept look, you also save the trouble
of packing nail polish. Remember, every little bit of
weight reduced adds up.

ELECTRONICS

22. LUGGING ALONG ELECTRONICS

Electronics have a large role to play in our lives today. Most of us cannot imagine our lives away from our phones, laptops or tablets. However while travelling, one must consider the amount of weight these electronics add to our luggage. Thankfully smart phones come along with all the essentials tools like a camera, email access, picture editing tools and more. They are smart to the point of eliminating the need to carry multiple gadgets. Choose a smart phone that suits all your requirements and travel with the world in your palms or pocket.

23. REDUCE THE NUMBER OF CHARGERS

If you do travel with multiple electronic devices, you will have to bear the additional burden of carrying all their chargers too. Check if a single charger can be used for multiple devices. You might also consider investing in a pocket charger. These small devices support multiple devices while keeping you charged on the go.

24. TRAVEL FRIENDLY APPS

Along with smart phones come numerous apps, which are immensely helpful in our travels. You name it and you have an app for it at hand – take pictures, sharing with friends and family, torch to light dark roads, maps, checking flight/train times, find hotels and many other things. Use these smart alternatives to traditional items like books to eliminate weight and save space.

I get ideas about what's essential when packing my suitcase.

-Diane von Furstenberg

TRAVELLING WITH KIDS

25. BRING ALONG THE STROLLER

Kids might enjoy walking for a while but they soon tire out and a stroller is the just the right thing for them to rest in while you continue your tour. Strollers also double duty as a luggage carrier and shopping bag holder. Remember to pick a light weight, easy to handle brand of stroller. Better yet, find out in advance if you can rent a stroller at your destination.

26. BRING ONLY ENOUGH DIAPERS FOR YOUR TRIP

Diapers take up a lot of space and add to the weight of your luggage. Therefore it is advisable to carry just enough diapers to last through the trip and a few for afterwards, till you buy fresh stock at your destination. Unless of course you are travelling to a really remote area, in which case you have no choice but to carry the load. Otherwise diapers are something you will find pretty easily.

27. TAKE ONLY A COUPLE OF TOYS

Children are easily attracted by new things in their environment. While travelling they will find numerous 'new' objects to scrutinize and play with. Packing just one favorite toy is enough, or if there is no favorite toy leave out all of them in favor of stories or imaginary games.

28. CARRY KID FRIENDLY SNACKS

Create a small snack counter in your bag to store away quick bites for those sudden hunger pangs. Depending on the child's age this could include chocolates, raisins, dry fruits, granola bars or biscuits. Also keep a bottle of water handy for your little one.

These things do not add much weight and can be adjusted in a handbag or knapsack.

29. GAMES TO CARRY

Create some travel specific, imaginary games if you have slightly grown up children, like spot the attractions. Keep a coloring book and colors handy for in-flight or hotel time. Apps on your smart phone can keep the children engaged with cartoons and story books. Older children are often entertained by games available on phones or tablets. This cuts the weight of luggage down while keeping the kids entertained.

30. LET THE KIDS CARRY THEIR LOAD

A good thing is to start early sharing of responsibilities. Let your child pick a bag of his or her choice and pack it themselves. Keep tabs on what they are stuffing in their bags by asking if they will be using that item on the trip. It could start out being just an entertainment bag initially but with growing years they will learn to sort the useful from the superfluous. Children as little as four can maneuver a small trolley suitcase like a pro- their experience in pull along toys credit. If you are worried that you may be pulling it for them, you may want to start with a backpack.

31. DECIDE ON LOCATION FOR CHILDREN TO SLEEP

While on a trip you might not always get a crib at your destination, and carrying one will make life all the more difficult. Instead call ahead to see if there are any cribs or roll out beds for children. You may even put blankets on the floor. Weave them a story about camping and they will gladly sleep without any trouble.

32. GET BABY PRODUCTS DELIVERED AT YOUR DESTINATION

If you are absolutely paranoid about not getting your favourite variety of diaper or brand of baby food, check out online stores like amazon.com for services in your destination city. You can buy things online ahead of your travel and get them delivered to your hotel upon arrival.

33. FEEDING NEEDS OF YOUR INFANTS

If you are travelling with a breastfed infant, you save the trouble of carrying bottles and bottle sanitization kits. For special food, or medications, you may need to call ahead to make sure you have a refrigerator where you are staying.

34. FEEDING NEEDS OF YOUR TODDLER

With the progression from infancy to toddler, their dietary requirements too evolve. You will have to pack some snacks for travelling time. Fresh fruits and vegetables can be purchased at your destination. Most of the cities you travel to in whichever part of the world, will have baby food products and formulas, available at the local drug-store or the supermarket.

35. PICKING CLOTHES FOR YOUR BABY

Contrary to popular belief, babies can do without many changes of clothes. At the most pack 2 outfits per day. Pack mix and match type clothes for your little one as well. Pick things which are comfortable to wear and quick to dry.

36. SELECTING SHOES FOR YOUR BABY

Like outfits, kids can make do with two pairs of comfortable shoes. If you can get some water resistant shoes it will be best. To expedite drying wet shoes, you can stuff newspaper in them then wrap them with newspaper and leave them to dry overnight.

37. KEEP ONE CHANGE OF CLOTHES HANDY

Travelling with kids can be tricky. Keep a change of clothes for the kids and mum handy in your purse or tote bag. This takes a bit of space in your hand luggage but comes extremely handy in case there are any accidents or spills.

38. LEAVE BEHIND BABY ACCESSORIES

Baby accessories like their bed, bath tub, car seat, crib etc. should be left at home. Many hotels provide a crib on request, while car seats can be borrowed from friends or rented. Babies can be given a bath in the hotel sink or even in the adult bath tub with a little bit of water. If you bring a few bath toys, they can be used in the bath, pool, and out of water. They can also be sanitized easily in the sink.

39. CARRY A SMALL LOAD OF PLASTIC BAGS

With children around there are chances of a number of soiled clothes and diapers. These plastic bags help to sort the dirt from the clean inside your big bag.

These are very light weight and come in handy to other carry stuff as well at times.

PACK WITH A PURPOSE

40. PACKING FOR BUSINESS TRIPS

One neutral-colored suit should suffice. It can be paired with different shirts, ties and accessories for different occasions. One pair of black suit pants could be worn with a matching jacket for the office or with a snazzy top for dinner.

41. PACKING FOR A CRUISE

Most cruises have formal dinners, and that formal dress usually takes up a lot of space. However you might find a tuxedo to rent. For women, a short black dress with multiple accessory options will do the trick.

42. PACKING FOR A LONG TRIP OVER DIFFERENT CLIMATES

The secret packing mantra for travel over multiple climates is layering. Layering traps air around your body creating insulation against the cold. The same light t-shirt that is comfortable in a warmer climate can be the innermost layer in a colder climate.

REDUCE SOME MORE WEIGHT

43. LEAVE PRECIOUS THINGS AT HOME

Things that you would hate to lose or get damaged leave them at home. Precious jewelry, expensive gadgets or dresses, could be anything. You will not require these on your trip. Leave them at home and spare the load on your mind.

44. SEND SOUVENIRS BY MAIL

If you have spent all your money on purchasing souvenirs, carrying them back in the same bag that you brought along would be difficult. Either pack everything in another bag and check it in the airport or get everything shipped to your home. Use an international carrier for a secure transit, but this could be more expensive than the checking fees at the airport.

45. AVOID CARRYING BOOKS

Books equal to weight. There are many reading apps which you can download on your smart phone or tab.

Plus there are gadgets like Kindle and Nook that are thinner and lighter alternatives to your regular book.

CHECK, GET, SET, CHECK AGAIN

46. STRATEGIZE BEFORE PACKING

Create a travel list and prepare all that you think you need to carry along. Keep everything on your bed or floor before packing and then think through once again – do I really need that? Any item that meets this question can be avoided. Remove whatever you don't really need and pack the rest.

47. TEST YOUR LUGGAGE

Once you have fully packed for the trip take a test trip with your luggage. Take your bags and go to town for window shopping for an hour. If you enjoy your hour long trip it is good to go, if not, go home and reduce the load some more. Repeat this test till you hit the right weight.

48. ADD A ROLL OF DUCT TAPE

You might wonder why, when this book has been talking about reducing stuff, we're suddenly asking you to pack something totally unusual. This is because when you have limited supplies, duct tape is immensely helpful for small repairs – a broken bag, leaking zip-lock bag, broken sunglasses, you name it and duct tape can fix it, temporarily.

49. LIST OF ESSENTIAL ITEMS

Even though the emphasis is on packing light, there are things which have to be carried for any trip. Here is our list of essentials:

- Passport/Visa or any other ID

- Any other paper work that might be required on a trip like permits, hotel reservation confirmations etc.

- Medicines – all your prescription medicines and emergency kit, especially if you are travelling with children

- Medical or vaccination records

- Money in foreign currency if travelling to a different country

- Tickets- Email or Message them to your phone

50. MAKE THE MOST OF YOUR TRIP

Wherever you are going, whatever you hope to do we encourage you to embrace it whole-heartedly. Take in the scenery, the culture and above all, enjoy your time away from home.

On a long journey even a straw weighs heavy.

-Spanish Proverb

PACKING AND PLANNING TIPS

A Week before Leaving

- Arrange for someone to take care of pets and water plants.

- Stop mail and newspaper.

- Notify Credit Card companies where you are going.

- Change your thermostat settings.

- Car inspected, oil is changed, and tires have the correct pressure.

- Passports and photo identification is up to date.

- Pay bills.

- Copy important items and download travel Apps.

- Start collecting small bills for tips.

Right Before Leaving

- Clean out refrigerator.

- Empty garbage cans.

- Lock windows.

- Make sure you have the proper identification with you.

- Bring cash for tips.

- Remember travel documents.

- Lock door behind you.

- Remember wallet.

- Unplug items in house and pack chargers.

>TOURIST

READ OTHER
GREATER THAN A TOURIST
BOOKS

Greater Than a Tourist San Miguel de Allende Guanajuato Mexico: 50 Travel Tips from a Local by Tom Peterson

Greater Than a Tourist – Lake George Area New York USA: 50 Travel Tips from a Local by Janine Hirschklau

Greater Than a Tourist – Monterey California United States: 50 Travel Tips from a Local by Katie Begley

Greater Than a Tourist – Chanai Crete Greece: 50 Travel Tips from a Local by Dimitra Papagrigoraki

Greater Than a Tourist – The Garden Route Western Cape Province South Africa: 50 Travel Tips from a Local by Li-Anne McGregor van Aardt

Greater Than a Tourist – Sevilla Andalusia Spain: 50 Travel Tips from a Local by Gabi Gazon

Greater Than a Tourist – Kota Bharu Kelantan Malaysia: 50 Travel Tips from a Local by Aditi Shukla

Children's Book: Charlie the Cavalier Travels the World by Lisa Rusczyk

> TOURIST

Visit Greater Than a Tourist for Free Travel Tips
http://GreaterThanATourist.com

Sign up for the Greater Than a Tourist Newsletter for
discount days, new books, and travel information:
http://eepurl.com/cxspyf

Follow us on Facebook for tips, images, and ideas:
https://www.facebook.com/GreaterThanATourist

Follow us on Pinterest for travel tips and ideas:
http://pinterest.com/GreaterThanATourist

Follow us on Instagram for beautiful travel images:
http://Instagram.com/GreaterThanATourist

>TOURIST

> TOURIST

Please leave your honest review of this book on Amazon and Goodreads. Please send your feedback to GreaterThanaTourist@gmail.com as we continue to improve the series. We appreciate your positive and constructive feedback. Thank you.

METRIC CONVERSIONS

TEMPERATURE

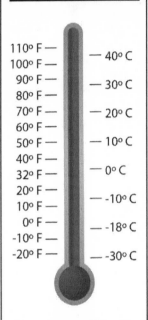

110° F —	— 40° C
100° F —	
90° F —	— 30° C
80° F —	
70° F —	— 20° C
60° F —	
50° F —	— 10° C
40° F —	
32° F —	— 0° C
20° F —	
10° F —	— -10° C
0° F —	— -18° C
-10° F —	
-20° F —	— -30° C

To convert F to C:

Subtract 32, and then multiply by 5/9 or .5555.

To Convert C to F:

Multiply by 1.8 and then add 32.

32F = 0C

LIQUID VOLUME

To Convert:.................Multiply by
U.S. Gallons to Liters................ 3.8
U.S. Liters to Gallons 26
Imperial Gallons to U.S. Gallons 1.2
Imperial Gallons to Liters....... 4.55
Liters to Imperial Gallons 22
1 Liter = .26 U.S. Gallon
1 U.S. Gallon = 3.8 Liters

DISTANCE

To convert ....Multiply by
Inches to Centimeters 2.54
Centimeters to Inches 39
Feet to Meters...................... .3
Meters to Feet 3.28
Yards to Meters 91
Meters to Yards 1.09
Miles to Kilometers 1.61
Kilometers to Miles............ .62
1 Mile = 1.6 km
1 km = .62 Miles

WEIGHT

1 Ounce = .28 Grams
1 Pound = .4555 Kilograms
1 Gram = .04 Ounce
1 Kilogram = 2.2 Pounds

TRAVEL QUESTIONS

- Do you bring presents home to family or friends after a vacation?

- Do you get motion sick?

- Do you have a favorite billboard?

- Do you know what to do if there is a flat tire?

- Do you like a sun roof open?

- Do you like to eat in the car?

- Do you like to wear sun glasses in the car?

- Do you like toppings on your ice cream?

- Do you use public bathrooms?

- Did you bring your cell phone and does it have power?

- Do you have a form of identification with you?

- Have you ever been pulled over by a cop?

- Have you ever given money to a stranger on a road trip?

- Have you ever taken a road trip with animals?

- Have you ever went on a vacation alone?

- Have you ever run out of gas?

- If you could move to any place in the world, where would it be?

- If you could travel anywhere in the world, where would you travel?

- If you could travel in any vehicle, which one would it be?

- If you had three things to wish for from a magic genie, what would they be?

- If you have a driver's license, how many times did it take you to pass the test?

- What are you the most afraid of on vacation?

- What do you want to get away from the most when you are on vacation?

- What foods smells bad to you?

- What item do you bring on ever trip with you away from home?

- What makes you sleepy?

- What song would you love to hear on the radio when you're cruising on the highway?

- What travel job would you want the least?

- What will you miss most while you are away from home?

- What is something you always wanted to try?

- What is the best road side attraction that you ever saw?

- What is the farthest distance you ever biked?

- What is the farthest distance you ever walked?

- What is the weirdest thing you needed to buy while on vacation?

- What is your favorite candy?

- What is your favorite color car?

- What is your favorite family vacation?

- What is your favorite food?

- What is your favorite gas station drink or food?

- What is your favorite license plate design?

- What is your favorite restaurant?

- What is your favorite smell?

- What is your favorite song?

- What is your favorite sound that nature makes?

- What is your favorite thing to bring home from a vacation?

- What is your favorite vacation with friends?

- What is your favorite way to relax?

- Where is the farthest place you ever traveled in a car?

- Where is the farthest place you ever went North, South, East and West?

- Where is your favorite place in the world?

- Who is your favorite singer?

- Who taught you how to drive?

- Who will you miss the most while you are away?

- Who if the first person you will contact when you get to your destination?

- Who brought you on your first vacation?

- Who likes to travel the most in your life?

- Would you rather be hot or cold?

- Would you rather drive above, below, or at the speed limited?

- Would you rather drive on a highway or a back road?

- Would you rather go on a train or a boat?

- Would you rather go to the beach or the woods?

TRAVEL BUCKET LIST

1.

2.

3.

4.

5.

6.

7.

8.

9.

10.